Original title:
Lemon Drops and Sunshine

Copyright © 2025 Creative Arts Management OÜ
All rights reserved.

Author: Arabella Whitmore
ISBN HARDBACK: 978-1-80586-380-9
ISBN PAPERBACK: 978-1-80586-852-1

Rays and Slices of Serenity

In a world of zesty cheer,
The wobbly sun brings good steer,
Juice spills from every grin,
Sour faces tucked in spin.

Giggles bounce like bouncing balls,
In sugar-coated sunlight halls,
A twist of tart, a splash of fun,
Who needs a cloud when you can run!

A Tapestry of Tartness and Bliss

A pie with zest sits on the rack,
With shimmering joy that won't hold back,
Each forkful brings a fruity bite,
Sour smiles dance in pure delight.

Beneath a sky of winking light,
The world awakes, it's quite a sight,
A sprinkle here, a dash of that,
Life's silly prance is where it's at!

Citrus Whispers in the Breeze

The air is sweet with laughter's tune,
As jester bees hum a funny rune,
Fluffy clouds burst into giggles,
While puns tumble like bouncing wiggles.

Sunkissed fruits hang on the vine,
Each squirt brings a tickle divine,
A jar of fun, a splash of cheer,
Taste the whimsy, crystal clear!

Radiance of a Golden Dawn

Morning rays dance on the floor,
While silly socks scatter and soar,
The world's a pancake, flat and round,
With syrup lakes that abound.

Wobbling laughter fills the air,
As sunrise drips from everywhere,
With smiles bright like morning's grin,
Join the joy, let the giggles begin!

The Shimmer of Citrus and Radiance

In the kingdom of zest where giggles roam,
Sour balls of joy make their silly home.
With a twirl and a bounce, they brighten the day,
Poking fun at frowns, in a playful display.

Tiny orbs burst with a bubbly cheer,
Fashioned in dreams where flavors appear.
They dance on the tongues of the giggling crowd,
Whispering secrets, soft but loud.

A Fresh Twist on Sunny Days

Beneath a bright sky, where antics unfold,
Zingy surprises, a sight to behold.
Wobbly jars filled with giggling delight,
Shimmery flavors, a playful bite.

Smiles scatter like feathers in the air,
Crafting concoctions that stir up a flare.
A twist with a laugh, they pop and they tease,
Bringing sunny chuckles with relative ease.

Golden Notions in the Garden

In a garden of whimsy, the giggles grow,
Tiny yellow treasures set hearts all aglow.
Each plump little orb, a jester's disguise,
Sprinkling humor in the warm sky's eyes.

Nestled among blooms, they chatter with glee,
Making light of the clouds that ever may be.
A flavor parade that prances around,
Mirthful bursts echo, a jubilant sound.

The Dance of Flavor and Glow

Charming the palate with a dance of zest,
Wiggly delights, oh, they'll never rest.
A whirl and a shimmy in every big bite,
Bringing forth laughter, oh, what a sight!

Frolicking flavors with a cheeky grin,
They wiggle and giggle, where fun may begin.
Every nibble a burst, every taste a giggle,
Joy in the air, watch it skip and wiggle!

Harmony of Days and Citrus Bliss

In a world where giggles reign,
Zesty bites of joy remain.
Squeezed from trees, a playful cheer,
Brightening hearts, bringing near.

Buckets filled with citrus glee,
Twirling 'round just like a bee.
Sun-kissed laughter in the air,
All our worries disappear.

Chasing shadows, running wild,
Like a frolicsome, free-spirited child.
Fizzing dreams in every sip,
Letting loose, a wavy trip.

Golden smiles in every bite,
Dancing day turns into night.
With each splash of twirling zest,
Life's a game, and laughter's best.

The Allure of Sweet Radiance

Twinkling joy in every beam,
Sugar-coated, it would seem.
Silly moments, oh so sweet,
Every corner, a joyful treat.

Bouncing in the afternoon,
Singing softly, a light tune.
Oh, the giggles and the sighs,
Wrapped in warmth, we touch the skies.

Brightened eyes and wobbly legs,
Wacky hats and silly pegs.
Dance around with glee so bright,
Making every moment light.

Laughing louder as we play,
Squishy smiles that fill the day.
With a wink and cheeky grin,
Let the fun and games begin!

Dappled Sunlight and Zesty Joy

In the garden where giggles grow,
Chasing shadows, just putting on a show.
Squirrels don hats, they dance and prance,
While flowers join in a silly chance.

Bees wear boots, they waltz in flight,
Blossoms burst, oh what a sight!
Laughter bubbles like soda pop,
In this zany place, we never stop.

Citrus-Laced Dreams in Twilight

In twilight's glow, we twist and shout,
Dreams of flavor are what it's about.
Orange sleeves and limey hats,
Join the fun, alongside the cats.

Juggling jellies, oh what a mess,
Sticky fingers, who can guess?
We giggle with the splashes bright,
Citrusy dreams take flight tonight!

The Opulence of Joyful Abundance

Sweeter laughter spills from the skies,
Where pie-throwing contests never die.
Frogs in bow ties croak funny tunes,
While fruit flies dance like fancy loons.

A banquet of joy served fresh each day,
With sprinkles of glee, we feast and play.
Joyful abundance in every bite,
In our funny world, everything's bright!

A Cascade of Sunlight and Flavor

A splash of fun in every ray,
Gather round, let's laugh and play.
Fruits in hats, how droll they seem,
In a whimsical world, we chase a dream.

Sunshine giggles, tickling our cheeks,
Flavors burst forth, oh, how it peaks!
A cascade of chuckles as we rejoice,
In our silly realm, let's raise our voice!

Melodies of Light and Tang

In the garden, bright and zesty,
Flavors dance, oh so testy.
Giggling fruits with laughter rife,
A symphony of zestful life.

Juggling colors, sweet and bold,
Wonders new, stories told.
With every bite, a chuckle spreads,
Gold and cheer in brilliant threads.

Bright Horizons of Citrus Delight

Morning giggles in the breeze,
Silly fruits jump with such ease.
Cheerful hues in every shade,
Nature's jest, a grand parade.

In bowls of joy, they roll and play,
Witty smiles can't slip away.
Each segment spills a burst of fun,
Underneath the glowing sun.

Sunshine's Sweet Embrace

With twinkling eyes, they shine so bright,
Funny faces, pure delight.
A splash of tang with every taste,
Giggles float, never a waste.

In sticky hands and sunny days,
Fruitful laughter fills the bays.
Around the world, their antics spread,
Making smiles where hearts are led.

Radiant Drops on Leafy Canopies

Dripping joy from branches green,
Nature's quirks, a lively scene.
Bouncing droplets, laughter loud,
In the shadiest, happiest crowd.

Every leaf a stage for glee,
Quirky fruits, wild and free.
Whisper secrets in the shade,
In this circus, fun is made.

The Taste of Yellow Happiness

A giggle from the kitchen, a splash of cheer,
Mixing up the zesty, everyone draws near.
Sour and sweet in each tiny burst,
A smile's full recipe, never rehearsed.

Laughter bubbles over, it dances and shines,
Fooling the taste buds with silly designs.
A twist of fun, like a jester's cap,
Life's a carnival in a citrus wrap.

Vibrant Hues of Daylight

Golden rays paint the kitchen bright,
Bouncing off walls, a playful sight.
A splash of zest in a wild game,
Chasing giggles, we're never the same.

Jars of colors, a rainbow parade,
A citrus circus, memories made.
Sipping joy from silly cups,
In a world where the laughter never ups.

Sparkling Mirth and Bright Citrus Chill

Fizzing in glasses, a bubbly delight,
Sipping the joy till we giggle all night.
Sticky fingers and sugar-high grins,
In this cocktail of joy, every day wins.

Squirting bright juice, we make silly faces,
Chasing each other through sweet, sunny spaces.
Baskets of giggles, laughter's refrain,
In this zany dance, we'll never complain.

Sunshine's Citrus Waltz

Waltzing through the garden in zest and cheer,
A choreographed jig with a funny veneer.
Green thumbs jiving with each little sprout,
In this sunny soiree, there's never a doubt.

Twirl, dip, and tickle, a playful embrace,
Fruity confessions, we quicken the pace.
With spritz of the tang, we toast to the fun,
Shining and laughing, we're getting it done.

Citrus Hues on the Horizon

In a world of smiles and zest,
Where fruit wears a playful vest,
A jester's folly on display,
Yellow jokes to brighten the day.

With giggles spritzed in every bite,
Sour laughs dance with pure delight,
Orange hats and green shoes sway,
As silly critters come out to play.

A Splash of Radiance in the Garden

In the garden, laughter blooms,
Bouncing high like colorful plumes,
A melon wants to join the fun,
While cucumbers roll under the sun.

With every jump, there's quite a scene,
Tomatoes dressed in emerald green,
Flavors burst, a tasty spree,
While carrots dance around a tree.

Golden Ribbons of Flavor and Light

A jolly twist of tangled vines,
Winks and grins from berry lines,
Twirling in a juicy spree,
As peas break out in harmony.

With every twist and every turn,
Fruits conspire, their colors burn,
Golden ribbons in a race,
Each one vying for more space.

Joyful Fusion of Bright Horizons

In a universe of sweet delight,
Citrus giggles take to flight,
Caught in bubbles, frothy dreams,
They splash around in syrup streams.

A merry band of taste and flair,
With silly stories to declare,
As cupcakes roll in fruity glee,
A tart surprise for you and me.

Sunlit Pathways of Sweetness

On a stroll through candy meadows,
Chasing giggles and soft shadows.
A squirrel with a bowtie prances,
As all around, joy enhances.

Bouncing bunnies with bright balloons,
Skip along to funny tunes.
Chirping birds wear silly hats,
While butterflies dance with acrobats.

Finding treasures under trees,
Like candy canes swaying in the breeze.
Laughter spills from every nook,
Across this sweet and sunny book.

Fragrant Drops from the Sky

Puddles filled with giggly squishes,
Dripping dreams and silly wishes.
Clouds chuckle in a fluffy choir,
As rainbows twist and never tire.

Jellybean raindrops splash the street,
Creating sprinkles under our feet.
We jump and hop with squeaky glee,
Oh, what a wondrous jubilee!

Cheerful clouds play peek-a-boo,
While dandelions dance in view.
Each drop brings a burst of cheer,
In this silly, sweet atmosphere.

The Cheerful Drizzle of Joy

A jester's hat spins through the air,
With every drizzle, laughter's there.
Mirthful splashes all around,
In this puddle of joy, we're found.

Cupcakes fall from the fluffy skies,
With frosting smiles and tiny pies.
We giggle as the fudge falls free,
A candy storm, what fun to see!

Ticklish rain on our eager skin,
Inviting us to dance and spin.
With every giggle, hearts ignite,
Mocking clouds in a sweet delight.

Luminous Trails of Zesty Hope

A path of sparkles leads the way,
With critters dressed for a bright parade.
Glowing trails of zesty cheer,
Guide us where fun disappears.

Merry daisies laugh and sway,
In this glowing, colorful display.
Bubbling streams of citrus glee,
Invite us all for tea, oh me!

With giggling frogs upon a log,
And dancing snacks that make us bog.
Each step is filled with bright romance,
As we twirl in this dazzling dance.

Breezy Notes of Sweet Bliss

A giggle floats on warm, soft air,
Where chuckles dance without a care.
Lemonade laughs, a fizzy cheer,
Tickling taste buds, oh so near.

Jolly breezes play peek-a-boo,
With citrus whispers, fresh and new.
Slip on laughter, a zesty breeze,
Joy rides high with such sweet ease.

Bubblegum clouds in a blue parade,
Mirth spread wide like sun on jade.
Forget your worries, float on by,
With each sip, let your spirit fly.

Silly hats atop every head,
In tasty dreams where fun is spread.
Life's a party, zestful and bright,
Welcome the whimsy, day and night.

A Canvas of Gold and Green

Brushstrokes of joy in bright gold hues,
Dance in the light, don't refuse!
Each cheeky grin, a work of art,
Crafting moments that warm the heart.

Skipping through meadows, laughter rings,
With colorful thoughts that feel like springs.
Footprints of joy in bright grass stains,
As giggles burst like summer rains.

Chasing butterflies, we set the tone,
Crafting uproar with every tone.
Canvas of laughter, giggly and grand,
Holding hands in a silly band.

Painting dreams with silly glee,
And tossing confetti in the sea.
Colors collide in a cheerful spree,
In this funny world, we all agree.

The Glow of Hidden Delights

Beneath the surface, secrets hide,
Bursts of flavor in a playful tide.
Pies and tarts hide precious smiles,
In every crumb, joy reconciles.

Tasting giggles, sweet surprise,
Candied jests in every bite.
Flavors sing in a joyous spree,
A mischievous laugh, caressed with glee.

Delight in corners, sneaky thrills,
With every nibble, the giggle spills.
Whimsical flavors taking flight,
In every layer, mischief ignites.

Cakes with sprinkles, oh what a sight,
Dancing flavors in soft twilight.
Sugar clouds and merry tunes,
Celebrating under silver moons.

Sweet Radiance on Summer Nights

Under the stars, laughter erupts,
Cheese and crackers in disco cups.
Sipping nectar, warm and sweet,
The silliness dances on our feet.

Fireflies twinkle, a playful game,
Telling stories, no two the same.
With sticky hands and grinning grins,
The fun begins where the night spins.

Chasing shadows in the warm glow,
Bouncing jokes, a teasing flow.
Breezy secrets, we share with ease,
Whispered laughter carried by the breeze.

As night unfolds with a playful jest,
In every moment, we feel so blessed.
Sweet radiance wraps us tight,
In a funny frenzy of sheer delight.

A Bottle of Joy in the Garden

In the garden, laughter sprout,
Where giggles grow, and doubts wear out.
Jars of cheer hang in bright view,
With zesty winks that chase the blue.

Bumblebees do a waltz or two,
Clowning around, they sip their brew.
A dancing breeze with playful charms,
Wraps joy around in sunny arms.

Frogs in hats, they sip and sway,
Making rain dances in a quirky way.
Petals chuckle, colors burst,
In this garden, joy is thirst.

So grab a bottle, take a chug,
With every sip, you'll feel the tug.
Of whimsy's whip and giggles' grace,
In the garden, find your place.

Warm Zest and Gentle Breezes

Where the warmth tickles your nose,
And tousled hair somehow just glows.
A gentle breeze with a wink and nod,
Whirling scents of cheer, quite odd.

Leaves dance chaotically in delight,
Chasing giggles into the night.
Each burst of laughter, a zesty tease,
Warming hearts like the sun—it frees.

Oh, playful shadows, what a prank,
Hiding behind the old wood plank.
Chasing sunlight with joyful flair,
In every corner, fun's in the air.

So bask in golden moments, my friend,
As laughter mixes with warmth to blend.
Sipping joy from nature's cup,
With warm zest, we'll never stop.

Golden Drops on Lush Grass

On the green, bright droplets gleam,
A silly dance, oh what a theme!
Frolicking ants in a joyous spree,
Celebrate with fruity glee.

Tickling blades of grass below,
Where laughter's fresh and habits grow.
Nature's play, a carnival spree,
Giggling under the old oak tree.

Squirrels leap and chortle loud,
In their antics, they're so proud.
An unexpected slip, a twist, a spin,
Funny moments never thin.

Each golden drop, a burst of cheer,
Sparks of joy are always near.
In fields of laugh and sunny class,
Find the fun on lush, green grass.

Vibrant Elixir of Light and Shades

A splash of color, what a sight,
In the garden, pure delight.
Swirling sparkles, a frothy plea,
Life's a mix of giggles free.

Bubbles popping, bright and bold,
In flavors that are stories told.
Sip the magic, laugh a ton,
With every sip, let jokes run fun.

Frogs wear glasses, take a look,
Flip-flops hopping like a book.
In hues of joy, we dance awake,
What a treat, for goodness' sake!

So gather round, friends, come and play,
Every moment brightens the day.
With vibrant hues to light your way,
Let's toast to life in our own way.

Whimsy in the Warmlight

In a world of zesty glee,
A pickle danced with glee,
The sun wore funky shades,
And laughed with a bumblebee.

Muffins wore tight pants,
As pies twirled in delight,
A cupcake sang a ditty,
Under gold's warm light.

Jellybeans jumped on clouds,
While cookies held a feast,
The laughter echoed wide,
From the greatest to the least.

Silly hats and bright balloons,
Decorate the cheerful day,
With every giggle shared,
In this quirky, warm display.

Citrus Galore beneath Azure Skies

A tangerine's wild dance,
Beneath the sky so bright,
With every twist and turn,
It kicked pure cloud-borne light.

The oranges told tales,
Of squirrels wearing hats,
While grapefruits giggled loud,
At the sight of silly cats.

In a patchwork quilt of fun,
The zest just would not stop,
As lemons wore mustaches,
And mangoes did the bop.

A toast to silly fruit,
In this sunlit affair,
Laughter twinkled like stars,
Fruity joy in the air.

Sunlit Harmonies in Nature's Bounty

The flowers whispered secrets,
To the bees in carnelian,
Who buzzed a little tune,
While waltzing with a radish, man!

A bubblegum cloud floated by,
Tickling the trees with joy,
Bananas played a symphony,
With a chorus of flying coy.

Cherries joined with laughter,
Swinging from the vine,
While peppers acted silly,
In nature's grand design.

With every note and chuckle,
The world became a play,
Filled with cheerful wonders,
In this merry, bright ballet.

A Tale of Citrus and Light

Once there was a citrus tree,
With dreams of being famous,
It hatched a plan to wear a crown,
And dance without any shame, us!

The lemons donned their tuxedos,
The limes wore sparkly shoes,
They twirled under a disco ball,
Choosing all the wacky moves.

A parade of fruit marched forth,
Bouncing in a jolly line,
While kiwi strummed a banjo,
Singing tunes that felt divine.

So gather round and join the fun,
In this tale of zest and light,
For every giggle shared today,
Turns ordinary into bright!

The Brilliant Dance of Flavor

In a world where sour meets sweet,
Joyful jigs on happy feet.
Squirrels laugh with a cheeky grin,
As candy clouds swirl and spin.

Pineapple winks, a playful tease,
While jellied frogs dance with ease.
Split a giggle, share a slice,
Every tang is oh so nice!

Fruits parade in colors bright,
Chasing shadows, what a sight!
In this carnival of taste,
Every moment's not a waste.

Bring your zest, don't be shy,
Let your laughter fill the sky.
Spinning flavors, make a splash,
In this whirlwind, feel the dash!

Chasing Light and Zesty Breezes

A twisty path through fields of cheer,
Giggling daisies, oh so dear.
Bouncing petals in a race,
With hints of zest and sunny grace.

Sipping nectar, bees all buzz,
Chasing dreams, just because!
A tickle sweet on every tongue,
As joy and laughter come undone.

Swinging from the branches high,
Breezy whispers pass us by.
Orange pops, they take a leap,
While mischievous goats hide in heaps.

Glee's the game, let's skip along,
As nature sings its merry song.
Capture moments, feel the zest,
In this symphony, we're blessed!

Gleaming Orbs of Delight

Round and shiny, what a thrill,
Dancing through the sunlit hill.
Bouncing light, they spin and twirl,
As giggles weave around in whirl.

Citrus faces, all aglow,
Join the party, come and flow.
A squishy hug from fruity cheer,
Whispers of fun are always near.

Buzzy bumbles, a clumsy crew,
Flavourful joy in full view.
As bubbles float on laughter's breeze,
Silly moments bring us ease.

Chasing after every spark,
With every giggle, leave a mark.
In this garden of delight,
We twirl together, pure and bright!

Sweetly Tart in the Afternoon Glow

In the sunlight, we all roam,
With tasty treats, we feel at home.
A sprinkle here, a twist of fate,
In every bite, we celebrate.

Sassy shades of green delight,
Burst forth bold in cheerful light.
Crunching laughter, oh what fun,
As silly stands make everyone run.

Wobbly jellies, open wide,
Giggling friends, we're side by side.
A festival of flavors bright,
As humor dances in the light.

So grab a scoop, don't be shy,
Chase the giggles, let them fly.
In this sweetly tart parade,
Our sunny spirits won't soon fade!

Sunkissed Drops of Happiness

In a jar, a squishy treat,
Full of zest, oh what a feat!
Sour smiles and giggles bloom,
Filling up each joyful room.

Tiny spheres of joy so bright,
Dancing in the morning light.
Sipping sweetness, can't resist,
Laughter's there at every twist.

Tasting rainbows, feeling spry,
With each quirky, funny try.
Munching on those sugary bites,
Silly faces, happy sights.

When your day is feeling gray,
Just indulge, come what may!
Sprinkled cheer in every scoop,
Join the giggle-sipping group!

Tangy Essence of a Cheerful Day

A tart surprise, a twist of fate,
Each bite leads to fun, just wait!
With a wink and playful zest,
Who knew sweet could be the best?

From yellow hills, the flavors flow,
With every giggle, smiles grow.
Poking fun, we share a laugh,
Tasting joy, a fruity half.

In cheerful sips and bubbly pops,
Happiness just never stops!
Bursts of cheer, in every taste,
Life is funny, none to waste.

So grab a friend, don't be shy,
Let the tangy laughter fly!
In this silly, sunny dream,
Every chuckle's like a beam.

Golden Moments in the Orchard

In fields of gold, oh what a sight,
Nature's prank with pure delight.
Little giggles hide in trees,
Whispers glide upon the breeze.

With each pluck, the laughter swells,
Fruity tales the orchard tells.
Sipping juice with smirks galore,
Life's a game we can't ignore.

Sun-kissed peels and winking eyes,
Crafting dreams beneath the skies.
Golden glimmers, sweet surprise,
Bumbling joy as time flies by.

Together in this merry spree,
Filling hearts with tasty glee!
Under branches, come and play,
For our giggles lead the way!

Fresh Beginnings under the Gleam

Morning's light with flavors fresh,
A comedic twist, oh what a mesh!
Waking up with silly songs,
Join the tune where laughter throngs.

Each sip dances on my tongue,
Life's a jest, we're ever young.
Mixing giggles in a cup,
Let's stand tall and laugh it up.

Sunshine bursts with zesty cheer,
Flavor fireworks, never fear!
In this comedy of tastes,
Laughter's never gone to waste.

So come along, let's make some zest,
Share the joy, you'll feel your best!
Fresh beginnings full of fun,
Here's to laughter, everyone!

Warm Rays and Zesty Dreams

In a world where laughter blooms,
Jokes are ripe like fruit in rooms.
Sunlight dances on the floor,
Zesty giggles call for more.

Tickling toes in citrus zest,
Sour faces at a jest.
Warmth in every cheeky grin,
Joy is where the fun begins.

A twirl of shades, a spark of cheer,
Taste the sun, it's time to steer.
Fuzzy slippers on the street,
Every step, a burst of sweet.

Golden rays that melt the cold,
Stories of the silly told.
Lively dreams that twinkle bright,
Citrus giggles take to flight.

Joyful Citrus Cascade

Splashing laughs like fruit from trees,
Tickled pink by buzzing bees.
Bubbly tunes in every nibble,
Sips of joy, we laugh and wiggle.

Citrus twists in bright parade,
Chasing clouds with jokes well made.
Every drop a burst of cheer,
Spread the giggles far and near.

Funny hats like fruit in spring,
Limey laughter makes us sing.
Dancing shadows on the ground,
In our bubble, joy is found.

Wobbling thoughts like jelly's dance,
Funny mishaps fuel the chance.
Brightened spirits, a vibrant show,
Citrus smiles just steal the show.

Melodies of Gold and Sweetness

Ticklish tunes in sweetness reign,
Dancing through the silly rain.
Golden sprinkles on our nose,
Joyful hearts in bright repose.

Cheerful songs of zesty glee,
Floating freely like the bee.
Melodies that twist and sway,
Laughing clouds and bright bouquet.

Our silly thoughts like candy twist,
Strange delights we can't resist.
Fizzy pops of laughter burst,
In the midst, we quench our thirst.

Joyful whispers, giggling sound,
Sweet adventures all around.
In this world where joy can bloom,
Citrus echoes fill the room.

The Brightness of Citrus Mist

A splash of fun, a spritz of cheer,
Brightened faces bring us near.
Dancing breezes, quirky smiles,
Fill our hearts for countless miles.

Lively pranks with fruity zest,
Ticklish moments at their best.
Punny jokes in playful air,
Float around without a care.

Clouds of laughter, sweet and bright,
Banter dances in the light.
Zesty dreams that pop and sway,
Whirlwinds of joy on this day.

Through this mist of giddy cheer,
Find the funny hidden here.
In the sparkle of the breeze,
Citrus giggles, hearts at ease.

Citrus Magic beneath the Sky

In a world of yellow cheer,
Sipping joy with friends so near.
Lime-green giggles round the bend,
Zesty laughter never ends.

Bouncing like a fruit confetti,
Squeeze the day, oh, keep it petty!
With every twist, a new surprise,
Smiles burst like golden fries.

Lemonade in twirls and swirls,
Dancing feet and laughing girls.
Oranges rolling in the grass,
Letting worries slip and pass.

In this tangy, vibrant land,
Every moment is well planned.
With a sip and playful rhyme,
We create our fruit-filled time.

Hues of Honey and Citrus Dreams

A splash of orange splatters bright,
With honeyed giggles taking flight.
Fruit flies buzzing—what a scene!
Sticky fingers, sweet and keen.

On a tree of candy zest,
Swinging high, we feel our best.
Taste the fun, the juice so wild,
Each drop counts, sweet and mild.

Sour faces turn to glee,
When the world tastes like a spree.
Dandelions dance in the breeze,
We're all laughing, if you please.

In the orchards where we play,
Every moment's fresh and gay.
With each twist, our worries flee,
Life's a punch of jubilee!

Enchanted Glow of the Orchard

In the orchard, where we romp,
Citrus giggles give a stomp.
Honeybees with tipsy flight,
Buzzing joy from day to night.

With a flick and zesty reel,
We make fun the biggest deal.
Fruits are bopping everywhere,
Laughter bubbling—light as air.

Orange hats and lemon shoes,
All the critters sing the blues.
With a wink and a sunny grin,
Strawberry hats make us spin.

In this frenzy, let us shout,
What this day is all about.
Join the fun, bring all your cheer,
Every taste of joy is near!

Sweet Drops of Delightful Glow

In a bowl of bright delight,
We swirl and twirl in sheer delight.
Fizzy sips and fizzy pops,
Every belly laugh just tops.

Pecan pies and twinkling eyes,
Mango smiles and pie-shaped lies.
Giggles run like streams of zest,
In this place, we are the best.

Splash of citrus, wild and free,
Juices flowing from you to me.
Caramel dreams fill the air,
Sticky sweetness everywhere.

Round the table, cheers abound,
Magic moments all around.
Life's too short to frown or pout,
So let's bring the giggles out!

Citrus Whispers in the Breeze

A yellow fruit that loves to tease,
With giggles found within the trees.
It drops and rolls, a playful sound,
In summer's warmth, it twirls around.

Sour faces, laughter bright,
Chasing shadows, what a sight!
Slice it up, add a twist,
Sweet chaos, none can resist.

Rinds that dance in the warm sunlight,
Tangled up in sheer delight.
A zesty joke upon the tongue,
In every bite, the fun is sung.

Oh, citrus joy, you spark our glee,
A burst of cheer, wild and free.
With every squirt, we shout and play,
And let the silly moments stay.

Golden Glimmers on the Tongue

A bright orb bounces, what a dare,
With cheeky zest and tangy flare.
Juggling smiles with every taste,
In silly games, we find our place.

Sippin' on giggles, never dull,
In jars of joy, our hearts are full.
Pucker up, we laugh and cheer,
These golden treats bring all the gear.

Fragrant breezes swirl around,
Chasing giggles without a sound.
Our playful hearts in summer's sway,
Find humor in the bright display.

Bursting flavor in the sun,
Each sip's a prank, a tasty pun.
Life's a joke when fruit's in hand,
Let's laugh together, oh so grand.

Dappled Rays of Zest

Bright beams shimmer through the leaves,
A fruity glee, the heart believes.
In sunlight's dance, we play a part,
With zesty bursts that tease the heart.

Bouncing laughter in the air,
Sweetly sour, without a care.
A zany twist upon our lips,
With every sip, the laughter trips.

Squirrels giggle as they pout,
"Where's our fruit?" they sing and shout.
The gleeful taste, a citrus song,
In summer's glee, we can't go wrong.

Gleeful bites, the rays that play,
In fruity bliss, we greet the day.
With dappled light and zesty cheer,
We'll laugh together, bringing near.

Sweet Acid and Summer's Embrace

Tangy giggles, oh what a mix,
In summer sunshine, we play our tricks.
With each bright bite, the laughter roars,
As we dance on the kitchen floors.

A splash of fun upon the tongue,
With fruity wonder, we are young.
Squishy squirt and playful jest,
We savor joy, it's simply the best.

Punny faces, twisted grins,
In every drop, the joy begins.
We savor sweetness with a pout,
In every squeeze, we scream and shout.

So toss that fruit, let laughter soar,
With sunshine gold, we crave for more.
In silly moments, we entwine,
With playful bites, our hearts combine.

Daring Citrus Adventures in Spirit

In a world where fruit can fly,
I once saw a lemon in the sky.
It wore a hat, oh what a sight,
Daring the clouds to join in flight.

With a splash and a twist, they danced in glee,
Spinning around, just like a bee.
Fruits in a conga, full of cheer,
Chasing rainbows, never fear!

A zesty crew with tricks galore,
Playing hopscotch on the store.
Juggling oranges, what a show!
Who knew fruit had such a glow?

In this quest for fun and zest,
We squeezed our laughs and took a rest.
For the best adventures, just remember,
A little fruit can spark your splendor!

Dreamy Meadows of Bright Elation

In a meadow where colors bloom,
Bouncing berries chase away gloom.
With each hop, they giggle and sway,
Creating laughter along the way.

Daisies dance, a vibrant jig,
While cherries play a game so big.
Kites made of fruit drift on high,
Painting the canvas of the sky.

A watermelon rode a breeze so light,
Whispered secrets to the night.
The grass tickled feet with its charm,
Nature embraced, spreading warm calm.

As the sun dips low, the fruit friends cheer,
The sweetest dreams, they draw near.
In this joyous field, we find our play,
Where laughter reigns, come what may!

Nature's Cheer by the Warm Glow

By the glow of a quirky tree,
Bananabirds tweet merrily.
With a swing and a sway, they take flight,
Painting the dusk with pure delight.

A juicy breeze tickles my nose,
As citrus sprightly begins to pose.
Nuts in a line, they sit and chat,
Debating colors, how 'bout that?

Grapes gossip about the day's fun,
Swapping tales of who's number one.
As fireflies join with a twinkling race,
Nature's cheer fills this bright space.

With each giggle, the night grows bright,
A festival of joy in the moonlight.
So come along, let's laugh and sing,
In this warm glow, happiness springs!

The Essence of Joy in Every Sip

Sip, sip hooray, the flavors swirl,
A fizzy punch makes my head twirl.
With a splash and a pop, it greets the day,
Bubbles giggle, come what may.

Straws like umbrellas in a joyful race,
Dancing in cups, they find their place.
Sipping slowly, oh what a thrill,
Fruity concoctions, what a chill!

The rainbow drinks hold secrets sweet,
With each drop, they bring a treat.
Juicy smiles in every gulp,
A playful twist, here's the result!

So lift your glass, let's make a toast,
To flavors that we love the most.
In this fun-filled drink parade,
Joy is served, let's celebrate!

Harvest of Brightness and Flavor

In fields of yellow glee,
The harvest dances free,
With laughter in the air,
And fruity dreams to share.

Beneath the giggling tree,
The chimes of joy decree,
That every zesty bite,
Will make your heart take flight.

A splash of vibrant zest,
Is surely for the best,
So grab your basket tight,
And savor pure delight.

When drizzled in good cheer,
Each flavor drawing near,
With every sunny smile,
Life's bliss is worth the while.

Blissful Drops in Warm Embrace

With splashes of bright cheer,
And giggles drawing near,
A twist of citrus joy,
Transforms each girl and boy.

In breezy laughter's wake,
We dance for fun's own sake,
As pops of joy explode,
Along this merry road.

Each drop a burst of bliss,
In every gooey kiss,
As sweetness fills the day,
And worries drift away.

With warmth that brings a grin,
The playful races begin,
In a garden full of tease,
We sip our life with ease.

Sunlit Serenade of Golden Fruits

A melody of cheer,
In every fruit that's near,
With whispers in the breeze,
As happy as you please.

Beneath the bright, warm rays,
We frolic through the days,
With zesty tunes to sing,
As joy becomes the king.

Each spark of golden hue,
Brings giggles shining through,
The sweetness we embrace,
Will paint a smiling face.

A serenade of fun,
We laugh with everyone,
As flavors dance and sway,
In sunshine's bright array.

Citrus Kisses on a Warm Wind

On breezes soft and light,
The citrus kisses bright,
A playful gust, oh dear,
Will make the worries clear.

With every rounded slice,
We find our hearts entice,
To laughter's sunny tune,
Beneath the laughing moon.

The giggles intertwine,
As flavors sweetly shine,
In every vibrant swirl,
The joy begins to twirl.

So come and dance along,
With zestful, cheerful song,
For in this sunny spree,
We find wild jubilee.

Sunshine Drifting through Citrus Grove

Twisting tubes of marmalade,
Giggles float like juicy shade.
A garden dance with funny smells,
Where every zesty story dwells.

Bees in bow ties sippin' tea,
Tickled petals, oh so free!
Squirrels juggling ripe delights,
Underneath those golden lights.

Oranges wear a silly grin,
As they play a game of skin.
Breezes whisper wacky tunes,
For a laugh, there's never noon!

Lemons rolling with great delight,
Chasing shadows, oh what a sight!
In this grove so filled with cheer,
Every fruit seems to persevere!

The Brightness of Joyful Days

Pineapple hats and mango shoes,
Dancing clouds in citrus hues.
Each morning brings a silly prize,
With a wink and a sweet surprise.

Frisky limes on swings they play,
Sipping fizz in a funny way.
Joyful birds sing silly songs,
As they flit through all day long.

Marigold mischief in the air,
Sunbeams playing without a care.
On these bright and zany days,
Laughter's never far away.

Giggling fruits in wobbly rows,
Tickle each other's funny toes.
To enjoy the gleeful rays,
We find joy in silly ways!

A Symphony of Light and Lemony Bliss

Here in zestful orchestras,
Citrus plays with sweet pizazz.
Lemons laugh in perfect time,
Dancing to a zesty rhyme.

Bananas with a cheeky toss,
Spinning tales of tangy gloss.
Crisp and crooning, even lime,
Joins the fun, creating prime.

Sweetest notes upon the breeze,
Bouncing 'round with quirky ease.
Citrus serenades abound,
Tickling us from all around.

With a splash of bright delight,
We shall party day and night.
In this fruity, joyful bliss,
We'll dance until we can't miss!

Sunlit Gardens and Bright Delights

In gardens where the giggles bloom,
Citrus chatter lifts the gloom.
Marshmallow clouds dressed in gold,
Playful tales from young and old.

Bouncing berries joined for fun,
With colanders of shiny sun.
Fruits in armor, brave and bold,
Guarding laughs and stories told.

Flowers sporting witty hats,
Wobbling like some funny cats.
They share jokes that twist and twine,
In this bright and silly vine.

On these paths of sour and sweet,
We find laughter, what a treat!
Every moment full of cheer,
As we dance, the joys come near!

A Dance of Citrus and Light

Beneath the twist of yellow glee,
Sour cheeks giggle in harmony.
Twinkling rays in a zesty swirl,
Dancing whims, a joyful whirl.

In the market, giggles rise,
Fruity jests in warm guise.
With a hop and a skip, they play,
Chasing worries far away.

A splash of tang and burst of cheer,
Every twirl brings laughter near.
Whisked away by vibrant tastes,
Sweet and tart, no time to waste.

Lemons waltz on sunlit beams,
Creating sparkles, tossing dreams.
With every sip, our spirits soar,
In this dance, who could ask for more?

Sunbeams and Tangy Sweets

Sunlit giggles sprinkle the street,
Ticklish laughter, a fruity treat.
Pops of joy in every bite,
Tasting the day, everything's right.

Zesty pranks in a citrus jar,
Chasing shadows, we've come so far.
Candy laughter, oh what a sight,
Tickling noses, pure delight!

Bouncing flavors in the air,
Sour tangs, no room for care.
Frolicking playmates, come one, come all,
Piling sunshine, we'll never fall.

In the burst of a shared good cheer,
Every giggle draws us near.
A symphony of sweet good vibes,
Dancing through our funny jibes.

The Glow of Citrus Serenity

A sun-kissed aura tickles the soul,
Fizzy giggles make the world whole.
With every sip, a burst of fun,
Shining bright, the day has begun.

Peeled laughter hangs from tree to tree,
Silly whispers set our hearts free.
Wobbly notes of sweetened cheer,
In playful banter, it's all clear.

A cheerful jig on a balmy breeze,
Sassy fruits bring us to our knees.
Bubbling sunshine, laughter contained,
In the glow, none are restrained.

Flavorful dreams take flight today,
Sparking joy in a fun-filled way.
With every sunbeam, our spirits reach,
Life's simple pleasures, that's our speech.

Glimmers of Joy in the Afternoon

Frothy wonders in a golden cup,
Tart giggles as we lift it up.
Twinkling rays play in our hair,
Every sip a sunny prayer.

With cheeky promises and zest,
Tasting life at its very best.
A frolic here, a laugh up there,
Lemonade dreams, we've got to share.

The afternoon whispers sweet delight,
Fruit-filled jokes make our hearts light.
Bounces and skips on the green grass,
In every wink, our cares don't last.

Giggling shadows under the trees,
Happiness dances in the breeze.
With splashes of citrus, we enjoy,
In this moment, we're all a joy.

Radiant Slices of Joy

A yellow fruit with a zest,
It rolls around, the life of the fest.
With each little squirt, a giggle erupts,
Sour and sweet, oh how it disrupts.

In salads it dances, a playful delight,
On cupcakes it shines, oh what a sight!
With capers and fish, it's quite the tease,
A tart little joker that aims to please.

Pour it on pancakes, what a grand scheme,
It turns breakfast into a citrusy dream.
With every bright slice, we cheer and we laugh,
Life's little pranks served fresh like a calf.

So raise up your cups, let's toast to this fun,
For life's zesty wonders have only begun.
Pucker your lips and smile like a star,
For joy in the twist is never too far.

Twinkling Citrus Dreams

In a garden of giggles, a bundle of glee,
Where bright little orbs hang high on the tree.
They bounce and they bob, in the warm sunny rays,
Spreading sweet mischief in oh-so-fun ways.

With a splash of delight, they dance on your plate,
A twist of the tongue, they never hesitate.
They whisper in secrets, so sweet and so sly,
With a twinkle of joy, they leap towards the sky.

When life feels too bitter, just pop one right in,
A burst of bright laughter, a gleeful win-win.
They'll spritz and they'll squirt, like playful old friends,
Creating a whirl where the humor transcends.

So let's gather 'round, with a chuckle and cheer,
For the tangy delights that bring joy ever near.
With a wink and a grin, we shout out with glee,
For the twinkle of zests brings out silly esprit!

Sunshine's Tangy Kiss

A splash of brightness, like a joke from above,
It tickles your senses, it fits like a glove.
This playful concoction, a giggle ensues,
With a tangy embrace, we joyfully muse.

In fizzy drinks sparkles, it plays such a role,
Turning sips into laughter, it captures the soul.
Like the sun's little wink on a frosty cold morn,
It bursts on your tongue, makes the dreary feel worn.

On pancakes, it spins tales of sweetness and flair,
While sneaky its splash, like a cat with no care.
With pies baked with joy, we gather in crowds,
For moments like these, we're wonderfully loud.

So gather your friends, let's dance in a swirl,
For life's tangy kisses, they ring like a pearl.
With laughter and cheer, we lift up a glass,
To the zesty surprises that help good times amass!

Bright Springs and Bitter Twists

With a curl and a whirl, this zesty delight,
Fills our hearts with laughter, a playful bite.
In puddles of joy, we splash right along,
With every bright twist, life sings us a song.

The wrinkles on fruit are like giggles in disguise,
It throws out its puns, then sparkles and flies.
On sunny old days, when the clouds hide away,
Its charm lights the path, making bright what's decay.

A dance on the tongue, a grinning parade,
With hints of pure mischief, it's brightly displayed.
So let's take a chance and twirl with the zest,
For life's cheeky flavors are truly the best.

Raise high all your glasses, let's toast to the jest,
In a world full of sweetness, find humor's behest.
With laughter that bounces through moments we bake,
We relish each twist, for life's just a cake!

Sweet Sours in the Morning Light

Woke up with a grin, oh so wide,
But I tripped on a pancake, what a ride!
Syrup's flying, a sticky surprise,
Even my toast wears a sweet disguise.

Coffee's strong, but my aim is weak,
Spilled my drink, now I hear it squeak.
Laughing at breakfast, what a show,
Turns out, last night I danced with a dough.

The cat gives me a puzzled stare,
As I wear cereal like I just don't care.
Honey's buzzing, the toast's in the sky,
Maybe next time, I'll just eat pie.

Morning giggles, with crumbs in my hair,
Today's a circus, oh I declare!
Sweet sours make laughter take its flight,
Each mishap shines bright in the morning light.

Sunlit Zest of Joy

A zesty spark in the afternoon breeze,
Squeezed a citrus, oh, if you please!
Tripped on the peels, landed with flair,
Even my shadows burst out in prayer.

On a picnic blanket, I lost my grip,
Rolling the fruit, oh what a trip!
The dog's joined in, chasing the chase,
While ants hold a feast in a wild race.

Lemonade's spilled, making puddles to splash,
My friends and I dive in with a crash.
Giggles erupt, as we slip all around,
What a zesty joy we've so brightly found!

Sun smiles down on our silly mess,
Nature's confetti, we simply confess.
Each moment's a treasure, pure and coy,
In this summer's light, we savor our joy.

Amber Hues and Citrus Dreams

In a grove of gold, laughter takes flight,
Chasing squirrels under skies so bright.
Citrus dreams dance on the warm breeze,
We tickle the oranges, oh what a tease!

Sipped sweet nectar, as bright as the sun,
But found a bee that thought it was fun.
With a buzz and a laugh, off we ran,
Chasing our giggles, the bee flew, oh man!

Picnic antics with jokes in each mouthful,
My sandwich jumped and declared it would twirl.
Under amber hues, laughter's the game,
Each fruity adventure ignites our fame.

With citrus sighs and a zestful gleam,
We're all just kids in this wild dream.
Amber hues spark mischief like a gleam,
In the orchard, we've woven our theme.

Bright Reflections on Dewy Leaves

Dewy mornings, a gleaming surprise,
Reflections laugh back, oh how they rise!
Bouncing on leaves, like a silly dance,
Every drop twirls, given half a chance.

Caught in the moment, splashing away,
My friend slipped in, claims it's 'splash play!'
We're soaked, we giggle, with wide-open eyes,
Nature's joke caught under the skies.

Bright butterflies join our morning caper,
While flowers bloom, blooming in paper.
Twirling and swirling, like a wild waltz,
Nature's laughter spins, my heart exalts.

Bright reflections mirror smiles in glee,
Joy rides the breeze, playful and free.
Together we giggle, wild as a wave,
With dewy leaves laughing, oh what we crave!

Sunlit Citrusy Whimsy

A zesty smile, what a treat,
With every giggle, life's so sweet.
Squirrels dance on citrus trees,
While bees hum tunes that aim to please.

Frogs in hats leap high with joy,
Twirling in a dress, oh what a ploy!
Juggling fruits with silly flair,
Everyone laughs without a care.

Lemons roll down a grassy slope,
Chasing shadows, weaving hope.
The sunbeams tickle each little hue,
As laughter bursts like morning dew.

In this world of playful zest,
Let's dance and sing, be our best!
For every giggle holds a glimpse,
Of joyous moments and happy shrimps.

Afternoon Bliss Wrapped in Brightness

A quilt of light on grassy grounds,
With laughter echoing all around.
Pies float by on fluffy clouds,
Tickling noses, drawing crowds.

Bouncy balls of citrus cheer,
Roll down hills without a fear.
Bunnies in bowties hop so grand,
While ice cream cones escape the hand.

Giggles spill like soda pops,
Each sparkle brightens, never stops.
Sunbeams wiggle, jump, and jive,
In this dream, we come alive.

Silly hats on heads so proud,
Dancing 'neath a fluffy cloud.
Life's a circus with its charms,
Wrapped in joy, in funny arms.

Blissful Citrus Reverie

A world spun round in fruity taste,
With every moment, none to waste.
Citrus scents in the air swirl,
As canvases of oddness unfurl.

Wacky waves of giggly cheer,
Made from spritzes of bright flair.
Kites that zip and zoom about,
Chasing laughter, never a doubt.

In sunny spots, we skip and hop,
With joyous whispers that skip and plop.
Mischief brewed in playful minds,
A jolly bunch, forever binds.

Wind chimes tinkling like cheers with zest,
In the realm where we're all blessed.
Each catchy tune pulls us close,
A citrus dream we love the most.

Whims of Sunshine and Citrus

Sprinklers spray with giggles bright,
As children play in pure delight.
Jumping jests and creamy treats,
Life's full of jams and funky beats.

A parade of cheeky fruit parade,
Dancing to the sun's sweet cascade.
Grapefruits twirl with wobbly fun,
Jumping high, chasing the sun.

Juggling joys beneath the skies,
Where laughter blooms and never lies.
Sunshine spritz with every cheer,
A lively balm, let's all draw near.

Ticklish moments float like air,
With giggles bounced beyond compare.
Sippin' joy on sunny days,
In this whirl, let's dance and play.

Orchard Glow and Laughter's Echo

In a grove where giggles grow,
Fruit hangs low in a sunlit show.
Colors burst like cheerful shouts,
Every tree has tales and clouts.

Jars of joy and silly dreams,
Wobbling beetles share their schemes.
Beneath the leaves, a squirrel prances,
Dancing in absurd romances.

Buzzing bees hold court with flair,
While breezes toss with a tease in the air.
With every sip of cheery zest,
It's a party, come join the fest!

So let your laughter bloom and swell,
In this orchard, all's well; all's well!
With each giggle riding the breeze,
Here's a toast to fun with ease!

Serene Citrus Serenade

A ball of juice rolls down the lane,
Chasing away all the mundane.
With quirky fruit wearing silly hats,
And chatting birds who nibble on chats.

The daisies wink with playful beams,
While cheeky ants march in teams.
Where citrus whispers tales so bright,
Of jests and pranks from morn to night.

Giggles bounce on every breeze,
Like confetti scattered with ease.
In every nook, a joke resides,
While mischief in the orchard hides.

So come and sway with silly cheer,
Find laughter in the atmosphere.
For here, the fun's never out of stock,
In this grove, we rock, we rock!

Glistening Juices of Dawn

Morning dew, a sparkle parade,
With frolicsome breezes that never fade.
Citrus glimmers, a playful sight,
As jolly critters dance in delight.

Juicy laughter spills on the grass,
While skipping squirrels dash and pass.
Each branch whispers a silly tune,
Beneath the watchful eye of the moon.

With every drop that springs with glee,
Nature chuckles, can't you see?
It's a circus act on every tree,
Where even shadows shimmy with spree.

So raise a glass to a fun-filled morn,
With fruity giggles, we're reborn!
In this dawn, we come alive,
In glistening joy, we thrive!

Sweetness in a Sunlit Grove

In a sunny nook where laughter grows,
The world is sweet, as everyone knows.
Fruits giggle low with funny faces,
Spreading cheer to all the places.

The grass tickles toes in a fun ballet,
While buzzing bees lead the sway.
With meme-worthy fruit in riotous hues,
They laugh at veggies that feel the blues.

A parade of flavors, a sugary court,
Dancing oranges come in for sport.
Plum and peach play hide and seek,
As giggle-fests make everyone weak.

So let's savor this wacky ride,
With sweetness and laughter as our guide.
In this grove where joy is rife,
Let's celebrate the fruit of life!

www.ingramcontent.com/pod-product-compliance
Lightning Source LLC
Chambersburg PA
CBHW070007300426
43661CB00141B/273